HE MADE FUN OF ME

IGNORE OR CONFRONT?

You Choose the Ending

by Connie Colwell Miller • illustrated by Sofia Cardoso

Do you ever wish you could change a story or choose a different ending?

IN THESE BOOKS, YOU CAN!

Read along and when you see this:

WHAT HAPPENS NEXT?

Skip to the page for that choice, and see what happens.

In this story, John makes fun of Kurt. Will Kurt ignore the teasing, or will he confront the problem? YOU make the choices!

It's break time during Kurt's tae kwon do class.

"You really suck at this new pattern, Kurt," John says.

"I can't believe how terrible you are."

WHAT HAPPENS NEXT?

→ If Kurt ignores John, turn the page.

If Kurt speaks up, turn to page 20. ←

Kurt goes back to the mat. But John follows. "Didn't you hear me, Kurt?" he says. "You suck so bad you should quit."

Kurt feels tears welling up behind his eyes. John has been teasing him every week.

WHAT HAPPENS NEXT?

If Kurt confronts John, turn the page.
If Kurt keeps ignoring John, turn to page 16.

"Maybe I'm not as good as you yet," Kurt says,
"but I don't suck!"

"Whatever, dude," John replies. "You suck in my book."

TURN TO PAGE 18 →

"Shut up!" Kurt yells. "Stop picking on me!"
Master Daniels and the entire class hear him.
Everyone looks up in shock.

TURN THE PAGE →

Master Daniels makes both boys sit out for the rest of class.

After class, Master Daniels talks to the boys. Master Daniels suspends John from class for two weeks because of the bullying. Kurt is relieved. If it happens again, he'll speak up right away.

THE END

Go to page 23.

Kurt endures John's teasing the rest of class. He works on the pattern anyway and even improves.

But when the lesson ends, John says, "All that practice and you still suck!"

TURN THE PAGE →

Kurt's mother takes him out to the car. As soon as he gets inside, he bursts into tears.

"I don't want to take tae kwon do lessons anymore!"

Kurt isn't sure he will go back—not as long as John is there.

THE END

Go to page 23.

Kurt tries to bury his feelings. He is afraid and doesn't know what to do. John stands closely behind Kurt and continues teasing him.

"You really messed up that pattern, dude," he says, laughing.

WHAT HAPPENS NEXT?

If Kurt finally stands up to John, turn to page 8.
If Kurt buries his feelings, turn to page 12.

Kurt continues to practice the new pattern. John quietly teases him. Kurt only says, "I'm learning."

Before long, John gets bored and moves on, leaving Kurt to practice. Kurt is proud of himself for not letting John's words get him down.

THE END

Go to page 23.

Kurt is a little afraid, but he knows he doesn't deserve to be made fun of.

"It's a new pattern," Kurt says. "I think I did okay for my first time."

Still, John keeps taunting Kurt.

TURN THE PAGE →

21

Kurt tells Master Daniels what is happening. Master Daniels makes John do **30** push-ups and assigns him a new spot, far away from Kurt. Kurt feels safer now that he's involved an adult. Now he can concentrate on tae kwon do.

THE END

THINK AGAIN

- What happened at the end of the path you chose?
- Did you like that ending?
- Go back to page 3. Read the story again and pick different choices. How did the story change?

We all can choose what to do when people make fun of us. If someone made fun of you, would YOU ignore them, or would you confront them?

For the grown-up Kurt and John—C.C.M.

AMICUS ILLUSTRATED is published by Amicus
P.O. Box 227, Mankato, MN 56002
www.amicuspublishing.us

Library of Congress Cataloging-in-Publication Data
Names: Miller, Connie Colwell, 1976- author. | Cardoso, Sofia
  (Illustrator), illustrator.
Title: He made fun of me : ignore or confront? / by Connie Colwell Miller ;
  illustrated by Sofia Cardoso.
Description: Mankato, MN : Amicus. [2023] | Series: Making good choices |
  Audience: Ages 6–9 | Audience: Grades 2–3 | Summary: "In this choose-your-
own-ending picture book, John picks on Kurt during tae kwon do class. Kurt
is worried and scared. Will he ignore John, or will he speak up? Readers make
choices for Kurt, with each story path leading to different outcomes. Includes
four endings and discussion questions."—Provided by publisher.
Identifiers: LCCN 2021056819 (print) | LCCN 2021056820 (ebook) | ISBN
  9781645492795 (hardcover) | ISBN 9781681528038 (paperback) | ISBN
  9781645493679 (ebook)
Subjects: LCSH: Interpersonal conflict in children--Juvenile literature. |
  Interpersonal relations in children--Juvenile literature. |
  Bullying--Juvenile literature.
Classification: LCC BF723.I645 M546 2023 (print) | LCC BF723.I645 (ebook)
  | DDC 158.2/5083--dc23/eng/20211217
LC record available at https://lccn.loc.gov/2021056819
LC ebook record available at https://lccn.loc.gov/2021056820

Editor: Rebecca Glaser
Series Designer: Kathleen Petelinsek
Book Designer: Catherine Berthiaume

ABOUT THE AUTHOR

Connie Colwell Miller is a writer, editor, and instructor who lives in Le Sueur, Minnesota, with her four children. She has written over 100 books for young children. She likes to tell stories to her kids to teach them important life lessons.

ABOUT THE ILLUSTRATOR

Sofia Cardoso is a Portuguese children's book illustrator, designer, and foodie, whose passion for illustration goes all the way back to her childhood years. Using a mix of both traditional and digital methods, she now spends her days creating whimsical illustrations, full of color and young characters that aim to inspire joy and creativity in both kids and kids at heart.